Arms & Armour

IN TUDOR & STUART LONDON

The London Museum

M. R. Holmes, FSA

London: Her Majesty's Stationery Office 1970

Contents

Arms and Armour in London

COVER DESIGN
Detail of field sword late 16th century
See page 31

The Museum's collection of Tudor and Stuart arms consists, for the most part, of material excavated from London earth or dredged from the bed of the Thames. London-made armour is rare, and almost all the fine products of the Greenwich work-shops are already royal or national posses-sions in this and other countries, but the ordinary equipment of the sixteenth-century Londoner is well represented. Sword, dagger and hand-buckler were customarily carried by the younger men in their walks abroad, and are indicated accordingly, in illustrations like the costume-plates of de Bruyn and Caspar Rutz, and the group of typical citizens in the foreground of Hogenberg's map. (In the last-mentioned example, Plate 2, it may be observed that the figures have been reversed in the engraving, so that the older man is extending his left hand in greeting, and the younger one carries his sword and buckler at his right side.)

A certain amount of armour was preserved

in parish churches, not as a memorial to the dead but as equipment to be issued for use in an emergency, like the hooks and buckets kept there against an alarm of fire. Some such explanation may account for the presence of a characteristic Elizabethan breastplate (Plate 3), with a number of miscellaneous pieces of differing date and poorer quality, in an old farm-house on the outskirts of London. They would appear to have been cleared out of some church or other public building when the custom of having a regular town or parish armoury had fallen into decay. The description of Petruchio's wedding attire, in the third act of *The Taming of the Shrew*, suggests that town-armoury equipment was notorious for age and dilapidation, and it is to be observed that all the helmets are made with the skull in two halves joined along the crest, not forged out of one piece of metal as in the best examples.

Otherwise the Museum can show a fair selection of the arms in ordinary use. Two-handed swords, single or double edged, may be assigned to the beginning of the century, as may a curious fragment that may have been part of a ceremonial weapon, as the blade is not set centrally in the hilt, and the balance of the complete sword must have been peculiar (Plate 13). Excavation has yielded specimens of the long, swept-hilt rapier of the sixteenth century and the cup-hilted weapon of the seventeenth, and of the left-hand defences in current use with them. An almost complete leather buckler was found in Finsbury, and an elaborate central boss for a similar buckler comes from London Wall (Figure 1). It is noteworthy for its long central projection, which ends in a flat button instead of the usual spike. A well-known passage in Stow's *Survey* describes how 'The youths of this Citie also have need, on holidayes, after Evening Prayer, at their Masters doores, to exercise their Wasters and Bucklers: and the Maidens, one of them playing on a Timbrell, in sight of their Masters and Dames, to dance for Garlands, hanged thwart the streets', and laments the abandonment of these exercises in favour of less innocent amusements within doors.

As a means of parrying an opponent's blade, the buckler eventually gave place to the dagger, but the collection can also show one example of a less familiar alternative. It is a mitten-like piece of mail (Plate 14) which must have lined, in the sixteenth or seventeenth century, a glove for the left hand, so that the hand itself could be used for warding off a stroke.

For the latter part of the period we find rapiers, broadswords, hangers and seamen's cutlasses among the characteristic products

Fig. 1 Boss for a buckler, from London Wall

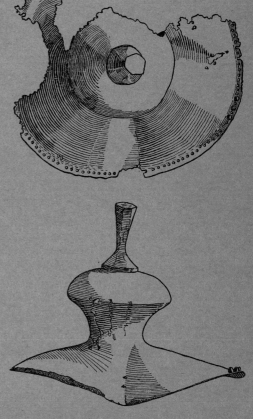

of the Hounslow sword factory. Prices and occasional specifications are given in a volume of contracts for equipping the New Model Army in 1645, in which, accordingly, we have a series of useful documents giving the names of various London tradespeople and particulars of the goods they supplied. The cartridge belt exhibited in association with a Cromwellian buff-coat corresponds so closely with the specification in the 1645 contract that we may safely accept it as one of those supplied at twenty pence each 'wth blew and white strings wth strong thred twist'.

The decline of hand-to-hand fighting led to the abandonment of armour as an article of general equipment, though the back-and-breast were occasionally retained by individuals who considered that the additional security was worth the extra weight. The helmet, however, survived only in the form of a metal lining to the broad-brimmed felt hat of the time. Such a lining is the small skull-cap of metal, with deep notches over the ears, which was dug up in Whitecross Street. It was at first thought to be an early Tudor piece, but complete examples in various other collections have shown it to belong to a period nearer the end of the seventeenth century.

The Greenwich Armoury

At the time of the accession of Henry VIII, England, almost alone among the great European nations, was compelled to go abroad for decorated armour of the type coming into ever-increasing favour. Helms of English make were well known, and a good many examples have survived, but, in the words of Mr. Cripps-Day, 'Of no piece of body-armour of the fifteenth or early sixteenth centuries still preserved can it be said that it was made in England.'[1] Contemporary sovereigns, such as the emperor Maximilian, the kings of France and Spain and even so near a neighbour as the king of Scotland, could make costly presents of armour manufactured in their own dominions, while the king of England was unable to make a similar return. It is not surprising, therefore, to find that Henry took pains, early in his reign, to establish a workshop of skilled armourers in England, and the Royal Armoury, manned

[1] F. H. Cripps-Day, *Fragmenta Armamentaria*, Vol. 1, Pt. 2, 'An Introduction to the study of Greenwich Armour', p 10.

by craftsmen from Milan, Germany and the Netherlands, was established in 1511 in temporary premises at Southwark and transferred to Greenwich in 1518.

The Tower of London contains armour made at Greenwich for Henry himself, and also specimens of the fine engraved suits for which this workshop was famous in the days of Elizabeth I, while in the Department of Prints and Drawings in the Victoria and Albert Museum is preserved the famous 'Jacobe Album', with its designs for the decoration of various complete harnesses with their extra pieces for use in the lists, or for fighting on foot. Some of the suits are white, indicating that they were to be carried out in bright steel, others are blued or browned, by deliberately induced oxidization.

Both styles are well illustrated by helmets in the Museum. The earliest is a russet 'close helmet' of about 1540. (Plate 4). The skull and the low comb are beaten out of one piece of metal; the visor, beaver and buffe, or chin-piece, are made to turn back over the skull on pivots and are held to each other by spring-catches, one operated by pulling a knotted leather thong and the other by pressing a stud near the upper edge of the buffe. A broad slot in the lower gorget-plate at the back presumably took a strap securing the helmet to the back-plate of the wearer's armour, and this detail, combined with the fact that the breathing-holes on the left side of the beaver are obviously later and more haphazard than those on the right, suggests that the helmet was originally made for tilting and subsequently adapted for the requirements of actual warfare. The plume-socket at the back appears to be a later addition likewise, and the helmet bears signs of further alteration for use as a funeral-helm, to be fitted with a wooden crest and hung over a tomb, probably that of Sir Nicholas Heron, in Croydon church, which was destroyed by fire in 1867.

The proportions of the skull and the profile of the visor are characteristic of Greenwich work, and are repeated in a later example (Plate 5), in which only the visor and beaver are lifted up, the buffe being divided into two hinged cheek-pieces to be secured with a hook in front of the chin. At the nape of the neck, on the left side, is a socket for a plume, and the neck is finished off with a cabled rim and a row of brass-headed rivets to hold the lining. The lines of the helmet, and the shape of the breathing-holes in the beaver, correspond very closely with those to be seen in the portrait of the 3rd Earl of Sussex at the Tower and in the armour of Sir Henry Lee, in the possession of the Armourers' and Brasiers' Company, and indicate a date of 1590-95.

A still later example is of bright steel, decorated with incised lines running across the head as well as following the main outlines. It is rather more crudely made, and was probably intended for use in the specialized conditions of the tilt-yard rather than the battlefield, as its breathing-holes are on the right side of the beaver only. The left, which would be the only one accessible to the opponent across the barrier in the lists, is designedly plain and unbroken, so as to afford no opportunity for a lance-point to lodge (Plate 7). The skull has been made in two pieces, and joined along the summit of the comb, an indication of its late date.

The general lines and style of Greenwich armour, which make it recognizable even when not adorned by characteristic engraving, are well shown in Hogarth's portrait of Garrick as Richard III, an engraving of which, by Hogarth and Grignion, is in the Museum's collection of prints and drawings (Plate 6). The breastplate is equipped with a lance-rest on the right breast, and is slotted on the central ridge to enable the grand-guard (the great reinforcing-piece often used in tournaments) to be bolted on when required. The helmet, even in its fore-shortened position on the ground, appears as a typical piece of Greenwich work, with a strong resemblance to the second example just described.

The change in methods of warfare which led to the gradual disuse of armour is reflected in the deterioration of the work of the Greenwich factory. The Dymoke Armour (Plate 1), impressive as it may look, is considerably inferior, both in material and in workmanship, to the examples already cited, but its very differences, apart from its peculiar association, make it well worthy of discussion. It is of bright steel, undecorated, and the helmet has the characteristic profile of the Greenwich school. The skull, however, has been made in two pieces and joined together less neatly than might be expected.[1] The separate gorget follows the lines of the gorget-plate on the helmet. Its borders of red trimming are repeated on the pauldrons and gauntlets, and all the appropriate pieces retain their linings of buff-leather. The helmet is padded with light-blue quilted silk.

The breastplate is still of the narrow-waisted type following the lines of the 'peascod' doublet of the previous century,[2] and shows some attempt on the part of the designer to preserve a certain elegance of outline. This fact points to a date about 1625-30, when the decadence had already begun, but had not got as far as the short-breasted style of about 1640. In this later style, the metal followed the not-too-elegant lines of contemporary costume,[3] and, being made for wear with riding-boots, stopped short at the knees.

In constructing the armour, careful attempts have been made to conceal the fact that the left leg is over an inch shorter than the right. The actual waist-line of the breast-plate is a little higher on the left side, and the screw for the attachment of the tasset is set higher and further towards the back, drawing all the leg-armour a little up on that side without a conspicuous shortening of any individual part. This peculiarity is of interest as showing how carefully such armour was designed and constructed to suit the individual who commissioned it.

This armour was handed down for many generations in the family of the Dymokes of Scrivelsby, and was traditionally supposed to have been worn by Sir Charles Dymoke when performing the office of King's Champion at the coronation of James II in 1685. The function of the Champion was to ride into Westminster Hall after the first course of a coronation banquet, armed in one of the king's best armours and riding one of his best horses, and to proclaim, through a herald, the new sovereign's right to the throne, challenging anyone present to deny it. The challenge would be uttered three times, and on no answer being given the Champion would drink the king's health in a golden cup and depart as he came, taking the cup as payment for his service. It has been ascertained that the armour worn in 1685 was claimed by Sir Charles Dymoke as part of his fee, but that it was in fact returned to the Ordnance Office and another engraved suit from the same armoury issued to him in its stead. The armour under discussion, as Dr. C. R. Beard has pointed out,[4] is more probably that used by John Dymoke at the coronation of George III in 1761, and the present linings, the gauntlets and the leg-armour below the knees (which is some fifty years earlier than the rest of the suit) would appear to have been added to it for the occasion.

The Greenwich shops appear to have been closed down in 1637, and this armour must therefore be one of the latest surviving examples of their work.

[4] *The Connoisseur*, May and June 1937. 'The Armours of the King's Champion' ,by C. R. Beard.

---

[1] Notably at the forehead, where it is normally hidden by the visor.
[2] London Museum Catalogue No. 5, *Costume*, p 24.
[3] *Costume Catalogue*, p 30.

The Armourers' Company

As has been stated above (p 4), the better quality of plate armour was imported from abroad during the fourteenth and fifteenth centuries. The English armourers, however, continued to supply the needs of the less well equipped, and to turn out helmets, mail and 'brigandines' of small iron plates covered with fabric.[1] The Armourers' Company of London had no mark of its own before 1590, and its mark is not, therefore, to be looked for on most Greenwich products. A good example of its seventeenth-century stamp of approval can be seen on the pikeman's equipment in the Museum. Here the crowned A of the Company (Plates 8, 9) is clearly visible at the neck of the breast and back, and on the border of the wide-brimmed 'pott' helmet, signifying that they have been tested and passed as serviceable by the Company's officials.[2]

[1]In the words of Mr. C. J. ffoulkes ' . . . the armourer of the early fourteenth century was a purveyor of clothing and equipment'. *Archaeologia*, 76, p 42.
[2]The test was made with a crossbow or pistol, as well as with a sword. In *Archaeologia*, 51, pp 167-72, is given an account of the testing of a pistol-proof Greenwich breast-plate.

The revision of military tactics which followed the improvement of hand firearms led in its turn to the gradual disuse of armour, first from the legs, in favour of high boots, and then from the arms and body, where it was superseded by the buff-coat. The only metal defence of the arquebusier by the middle of the seventeenth century was the 'Spanish morion'; the musketeer had abandoned even this, and wore a broad-brimmed hat. Hand-to-hand fighting was confined to the cavalryman and the pikeman, who consequently retained a certain amount of body armour. The horseman might wear a 'back-and-breast' over a buff-coat, or a more or less complete suit of plate down to the knees, with a 'burgonet', or crested, open-faced helmet with hinged cheek-pieces (Plate 10), while the pikeman would have back-and-breast, possibly, but not invariably, a gorget, tassets reaching to mid-thigh and a 'Spanish morion' or combed 'pott' (Plates 8, 10).

In 1685 the Company was given the right of search and approval of 'all edge-tools and armour, and all copper and brass work wrought with the hammer within the City of London'[3] and the consequent overlapping of the privileges of the Brasiers' Company led to the incorporation of the two Companies under Queen Anne.

[3]P. M. Ditchfield, *The City Companies of London*, p 178.

L.28/1 (Plate 4)

Close helmet of russet steel, with comb and skull forged out of one piece of metal. Visor with double sights separated by a ridge, beaver of characteristic Greenwich outline, pierced with breathing-holes on both sides, those on the left being irregular in arrangement and cruder in finish, suggesting that they were inserted later. Spring catches above and below, the upper one operated by a knotted thong, the lower by a press-stud. Buffe turning on same pivots as visor and beaver. Gorget-plates of two lames in front and behind, originally linked to each other by a stud and keyhole-slot on each side. Slot in centre of lowest lame at back, presumably to take a strap holding the helmet to the back-plate of the wearer's armour. Plume-socket at left side of nape a later addition, though nearly contemporary. Holes in comb and visor apparently made to take a crest-spike when the helmet was hung over the tomb of Sir Nicholas Heron (d. 1568), probably its original owner, in Croydon church.
Lent by the Parochial Church Council, Croydon Parish Church.

50.75 (Plate 5)

Close helmet of russet steel, with comb and skull forged out of one piece of metal. Visor with double sights and ridge, beaver of characteristic Greenwich outline pierced with breathing-holes on both sides and fitted with spring-catches above and below. Hinged cheek-pieces meeting at the chin. Deep neck-ring to fit over rim of gorget. Socket for a plume on left side of nape. Brass-headed rivets round neck-ring to hold the lining. Slight cable-pattern on comb, neck-ring and ridges of visor, and main plates bordered by double incised lines. Greenwich work, about 1590.

49.10/9 (Plate 7)

Close helmet of bright steel, with comb and skull in two pieces. Visor, beaver and buffe all mounted to turn up on the same pivots and held in position by hook-and-eye catches on right side. Visor with double sights and ridge, hole for a lifting-peg (now missing) on right side, beaver pierced with breathing-holes on right side only. Single gorget-plates in front and behind. Design of double incised lines radiating from visor-pivots. Greenwich work, about 1610.

L.28/2

Close helmet of so-called 'Death's-head' or 'Savoyard' type. Skull made in two parts riveted together, and ornamented with ridges and incised single lines radiating from a central pierced depression at apex, which may have once held a finial. Brow-peak, visor and buffe all turning on the same pivots. Peak very thin and crudely made, visor almost flat, with upper part of face left open except for a weak upright between the eye-openings, which would seem to have been cut out with shears. Irregular rosette piercings low on cheeks, and small lozenge-shaped opening opposite mouth. Buffe broken and repaired, but of much firmer construction and reminiscent of Greenwich type. Single gorget-plates, with simulated lames, added at front and rear, and quite possibly not belonging to the helmet. Crude hole for a crest-spike in front of skull. Whole piece much patched and mended, and likely to have been put together, possibly from odd scraps, for the funeral of Captain Nicholas Hatcher, who commanded a troop of horse under Charles I, became Yeoman-Usher in Ordinary to Charles II and was buried in Croydon church in 1673. *Lent by the Parochial Church Council, Croydon Parish Church.*

A.7658 (Plate 3)

Breastplate, with peascod outline and central ridge. Neck and arm-holes slightly turned back. Bottom flanged, with a broad skirt-plate riveted on. Two holes and a stud on each shoulder. Late 16th century. From an old farm-house near Ongar.

A.7665 (Plate 11)

Elbow-cop, originally made in one piece, but broken and mended again in the bend of the elbow-joint.
16th century. From an old farm-house near Ongar.

A.6419

Forepart of a vambrace, or defence for the arm, opening on a hinge and fastening with a spring catch. Three rivet-holes in upper edge.
16th century.

A.6415

Gauntlet for the left hand. Long cuff, open on the inner side, with cable border, slight central ridge and small boss over the wristbone. Back of hand covered by four plates.
16th century. From an old house in London.

A.6416

Gauntlet for the right hand, similar to the preceding example, and associated with it, but not a pair with it, being longer in the cuff. Portion of wrist-strap still attached, and the knuckle-plate retains the hinge of the thumb-plate.
16th century. From an old house in London.

A.11478 (Plate 11)
Gauntlet for the left hand. Short, wide cuff, slightly pointed and bordered with seven rivets one of which is missing. Back of hand covered by six plates. Knuckle-plate scalloped and indented for the fingers, and retains traces of the leather to which they were attached.
Mid 16th century. Found in Southwark.

A.3669 (Plate 14)
Mail lining for a duelling-glove, to be worn on the left hand.
16th or 17th century. Found in Worship Street.
Given by Sir Guy Laking, Bart.

A.5880
Iron shield-boss, rim much corroded, retaining two large rivets out of a probable five.
Early 16th century. Found in the Thames.

A.3705 (Plate 12)
Buckler made of two thicknesses of leather, joined by eight large rosettes of iron to a ring of strip metal. Rim of central boss still in position, and pierced for eight rivets.
16th century. Found in Finsbury.

A.15261 (Fig. 1)
Iron shield-boss with fragmentary beaded edge, large knob and projection ending in a button.
16th century. Found in London Wall.

A.16927
Rim of buckler. Incomplete circle of iron, double, with fragments of wood still held in place. Six rivets remain out of eight. Upper rim turned outwards at the circumference, and indented on the inner edge.
16th century. Found in London.
Given by F. Ransom, Esq.

34.121 (Plate 1)
The Dymoke Armour. Complete armour in bright steel with brass-headed rivets. Combed helmet with gorget-plates attached, two-piece visor and beaver all turning on the same pivots and fastening with a hook. Lower half of visor sharply pointed in front, pierced on each side with circular holes in a flower-pattern and stamped with a crowned M.R. Skull forged in two pieces and lined with light-blue quilted silk. Socket for plume at back of neck. Separate gorget, gauntlets and pauldrons all trimmed with red cloth and retaining their buff-leather linings. Long laminated tassets bolted to the skirt-plate, and later augmented with greaves and sabatons from an armour of 1575–80. Brass spurs (one broken, and both rowels missing) riveted to the heels.

Greenwich work, 1625–30. Traditionally given to Sir Charles Dymoke as 'composition' for the Greenwich armour worn by him as Champion at the coronation of James II in 1685 and claimed by him as his fee, but more likely to have been the suit worn by John Dymoke at the coronation of George III in 1761.
Given by the National Art-Collections Fund.

B.307-8 (Plates 8 and 9)
Armour for a pikeman, consisting of breastplate, back-plate and 'pott' helmet. Breastplate with central ridge, slight point at waist and broad skirt-plate. Breast and back attached to each other by metal shoulder-straps (restored) and hooks, and by leather waist-straps, of which traces remain. Pott made in two pieces, with combed skull, broad rim mended at back and socket for a plume at rear end of comb. All three pieces bear the proof-mark of the Armourers' Company. Mid 17th century.
Lent by the Ministry of Public Building & Works.

A.7657
Tasset from a pikeman's armour. Six lames, riveted together into one rigid piece for the left side. Topmost lame bears two buckles for attachment to the breastplate.
Mid 17th century. From an old farm-house near Ongar.

A.15503
Breastplate, with pointed waist and central ridge. One stud on each shoulder for attachment.
Mid 17th century.

35.65
Breastplate, with pointed waist and central ridge. Bullet-mark or proof-mark on right breast, mark of the Armourers' Company on left side below collar. Three studs on each shoulder for attachment.
Mid 17th century.

A.10449
Breastplate with slight central ridge and pointed waist. Border perforated for attachment of lining. One stud on each side of breast. Proof-mark of the Armourers' Company just below neck.
Mid 17th century.

A.7666
Breastplate, with central ridge and projecting skirt-plate. Right armhole considerably larger than left, to give play to the arm.
17th century. From an old farm-house near Ongar.

A.7663
Spanish morion, or Cabasset. Made in two pieces. Narrow brim, much corroded.
Early 17th century. From an old farm-house near Ongar.

A.7664 (Plate 10)
Spanish morion, similar to preceding.
Early 17th century. From an old farm-house near
Ongar.

A.7661 (Plate 10)
Burgonet, with hinged cheek-pieces. Skull made
in two parts, with a hollow comb. Several brass-
headed lining-rivets still in position. The right
cheek-piece is an early addition from a slightly
larger helmet of the same type.
Early 17th century. From an old farm-house near
Ongar.

A.7660
Burgonet, similar to preceding, but with cheek-
pieces missing, and with socket and screw over
the forehead for a sliding nose-guard.
Early 17th century. From an old farm-house near
Ongar.

The Sword and its Development

Only at the end of the Middle Ages does the
sword appear to be looked on as a defensive
as well as an offensive weapon, and only then,
consequently, is it associated with civil dress.
The medieval Englishman, if he decided to
wear a sword, put on a certain amount of
body-armour as a matter of course; but
under Henry VIII or Elizabeth I he would
consider himself well armed if he had his
sword and a dagger, or perhaps a small hand-
buckler. This change of ideas is reflected in
the development of the sword itself. When it
is no longer intended for use by or against a
man in full armour, the blade becomes
narrower and lighter, and the hilt is constructed to afford some protection to the hand, now
that the steel gauntlet has been abandoned.

For field service, the heavier weapons were
still used. George Silver, in his *Paradoxes of
Defence* (1599), mentions the usefulness of
the axe, bill, halberd and two-handed sword
'in battels, and where varietie of weapons be,
amongst multitudes of men and horses'. The

two-handed sword of which he writes is the English weapon, not so long as the great swords of the later German and Swiss infantry, but approximating to the weapons illustrated by Hans Burgkmair in *Der Weiss Künig*. 'The perfect length of your two hand sword', says Silver, 'is the blade to be the length of the blade of your single sword', and the difference in size is accordingly to be found in the hilt alone. A typical example is a sword found in the course of excavations for the Great Western Railway (Plate 15). Its blade conforms with Silver's regulation as to length—that when the sword-arm is drawn back the point should just clear a dagger held in the extended left hand—and is balanced by a long grip and heavy pommel. Two small lugs on the blade serve to protect the forefinger if hooked over the quillon to guide the stroke, and the blade itself is blunt for several inches beyond, so that it could be grasped with the left hand if circumstances required a shortening of the weapon. The use of such a sword is well illustrated in contemporary battle-pictures, e.g. on p 77 of the 1577 edition of Holinshed's *Historie of England*, where it is shown in the hands of a man also girt with a 'single sword' and buckler (Figure 3 on p 29).

A later type of fighting-sword, involving a curious mixture of styles, is to be seen in a weapon found in the making of the Thames Embankment (Plate 16, Figure 2). This sword, as befits a weapon for use against men in armour, has the heavy pommel and broad, double-edged blade inherited from the Middle Ages, but the hilt has the elaborate finger-guards of the rapier—quite unnecessary in this case, as the hand that held such a weapon would be protected by a gauntlet. Swords of this type are to be seen in military portraits of the time of Elizabeth I, and the piercing of the pommel for a sword-knot, as in this example, is a feature that appears to be common only in the last few years of the reign.

One early sixteenth-century sword in the Museum, though found in London, is not of English make, but is a characteristically continental weapon. It is a short, double-edged broadsword, with a wide pommel and large figure-of-eight guard formed by bending the quillons in an S-shaped curve. The Imperial eagle is engraved on an escutcheon on the grip (Plate 17). It was found on the north bank of the Thames near Scotland Yard,[1] and is probably a relic of the state visit paid to Henry VIII by the Emperor Charles V in 1522. The type is particularly associated with the German mercenary soldiery known as Landsknechts, and the wearer of this weapon may well have

[1] *Archaeological Journal*, XXXIII, p 92.

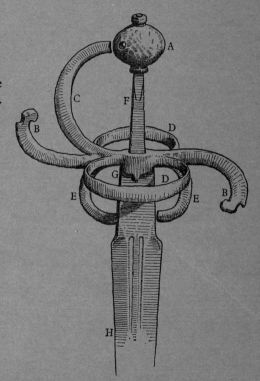

Fig. 2 Sword-hilt, late 16th century, showing the component parts

A. Pommel (pierced for sword-knot); B B. Quillons; C. Knuckle-bow; D. Side-ring; E. *Pas d'âne*; F. Tang of blade; G. Ricasso; H. Blade.

accompanied the Emperor up the Thames to the quarters assigned to the Imperial suite at Blackfriars.

The sword now worn with civil dress was rather narrower and longer, and had one or more side-rings on the hilt for the protection of the hand. The addition of the *pas d'âne* (see Figure 2) made it safe to pass the fore-finger over the guard, and other bars were added to protect the knuckles from a cut. In the left hand a buckler was carried—a small metal-rimmed shield which when not in use was hung at the waist beside the sword.

The remains of a leather buckler from Finsbury (Plate 12) show the usual type, and to such a defence, also, may be ascribed the metal boss, with its long central projection, which is also exhibited (Figure 1). This defence of sword and buckler is illustrated and referred to by various contemporary authorities, and was for a long time popular, but the gradual introduction, in Elizabeth I's reign, of the Italian style of thrusting with the point led to its disuse among the more fashionable, in spite of the protests of old-fashioned writers such as Silver and Camden.[1]

With the development of the thrust, we

[1] Shakespeare makes Hotspur speak of it with contempt when decrying 'this same sword-and-buckler Prince of Wales' (*1 Henry IV*, 1, 3), and the qualities of both styles of weapon are satirized in *Worke for Cutlers* (1615), attributed to Thomas Heywood.

find the old open guard being superseded by the cup-hilt of the early seventeenth century, covering the fingers more adequately from the attacking point, and when, later in the century, the introduction of the triangular blade marked the abandonment of cutting tactics, the cup was in its turn supplanted by a light shell which afforded all the necessary protection but at the same time gave the fingers greater liberty to control the weapon.

An early form of triangular blade goes by the name of *colichemarde*—a corruption of the name of the adventurer Königsmark, who was credited with the introduction of the style. Its characteristic feature is the abrupt change from a broad blade to a narrow one about a third of the way up from the hilt. This narrowing of the blade made for greater lightness and agility, and when it was found that a triangular blade could be narrow for the whole of its length without sacrificing its rigidity, the light small-sword of the eighteenth century had come into being.

With the change in methods of warfare, and the increased importance of mobility in the field, the soldier's armour and sword alike took on a lighter form in the seventeenth century. The horseman who wore half-armour only, or buff-coat and cuirass, required a firm blade for cutting and thrusting, but not the heavy 'bruising-iron'

of his ancestors. The metal gauntlet was laid aside, and protection for the hand was demanded from the hilt of the sword itself. A man on horseback had neither use nor opportunity for the nicer tricks of fence, and accordingly his sword, though it gave less play to the fingers than a walking-rapier of the same period, was better suited for giving, and parrying, the cuts of cavalry warfare. It was single-edged, and generally had a 'basket' hilt, a type derived partly from the cup-hilt and partly from the Venetian *schiavona*, and covering the greater part of the hand. Sometimes the hilt was adorned with medallions—a feature which gave rise to the theory that such weapons were memorials of Charles I, and applied the name 'mortuary swords' to the whole type—sometimes it was plain or, as in Plate 18D, decorated with a feather-pattern. This basket-hilt became characteristic of the Scottish broadsword of the eighteenth century, and the main characteristics of the type survive in the military dress-swords of the present day.

London sword-smiths worked on both kinds of weapons. Five rapiers in the collection are inscribed with the word 'London' and with the names of Peter Munsten and Caspar Fleisch, two smiths associated with Solingen in the Prussian

Continued on page 30

Plate 1 The Dymoke Armour (pp 6, 9)

1

Wynchester pk.

The Bowl car rynge

The Beare baytinge

Plate 2 Elizabethan Londoners, from Hogenberg's map (p 2)

Plate 3 Breastplate of 'peascod' form, about 1580 (pp 3, 8)

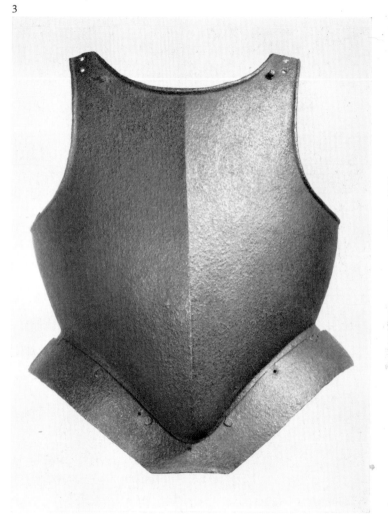

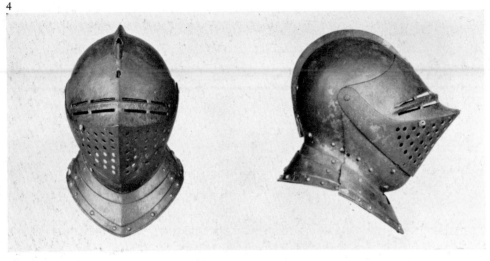

Plate 4 Greenwich helmet of russet steel, front and side view, about 1540 (pp 5, 8)

Plate 5 Greenwich helmet of russet steel, about 1590 (pp 5, 8)

Plate 6 Detail from Hogarth's portrait of Garrick as Richard III, showing Greenwich armour (p 5)

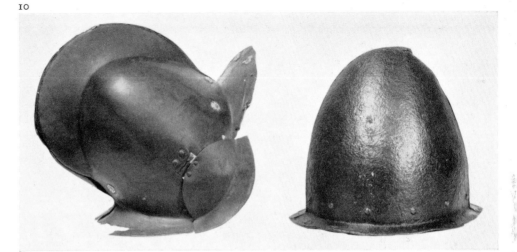

Plate 7 Greenwich helmet of bright steel, front and side views, about 1610 (pp 5, 8)

Plate 8 Pikeman's armour with London mark, mid 17th century (pp 7, 9)

Plate 9 The mark of the Armourers' Company of London (enlarged 3 times) from the helmet illustrated in Plate 8 (pp 7, 9)

Plate 10 Burgonet and 'Spanish morion', about 1600 (pp 7, 10)

Plate 11 Gauntlet and elbow-cop, 16th century (pp 8, 9)

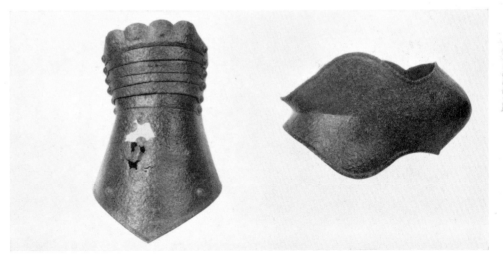

Plate 12 Leather buckler from Finsbury (pp 3, 9)

Plate 13 Fragment of sword with eccentric blade
(pp 3, 30)

Plate 14 Mail lining for a duelling-glove (pp 3, 9)

13

14

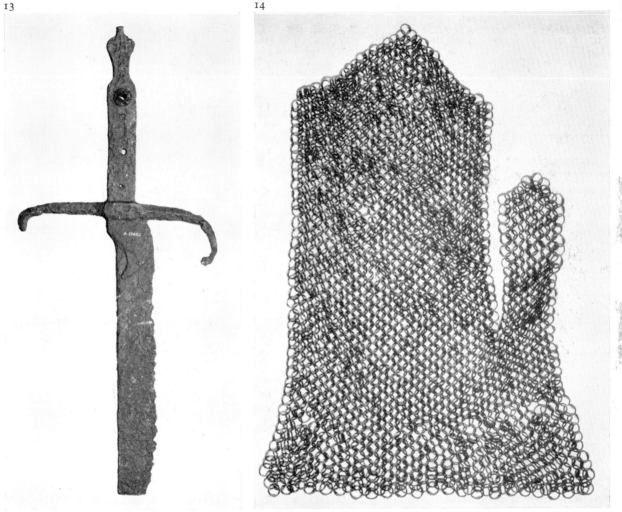

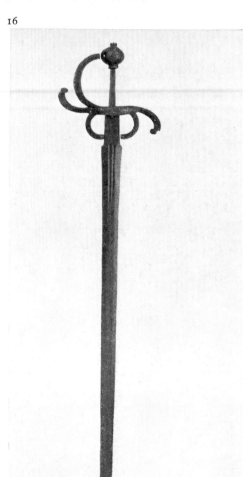

Plate 15 Two-handed sword, early 16th century. Length over all, 56 in. (pp 11, 31)

Plate 16 Field sword, late 16th century. Length over all, 40 in. (pp 11, 31)

Plate 17 Hilt of 'Landsknecht' sword, about 1520 (pp 11, 30)

Plate 18 Four London-made sword-hilts, showing the transition from the cup to the basket type (pp 12, 31, 35, 36)

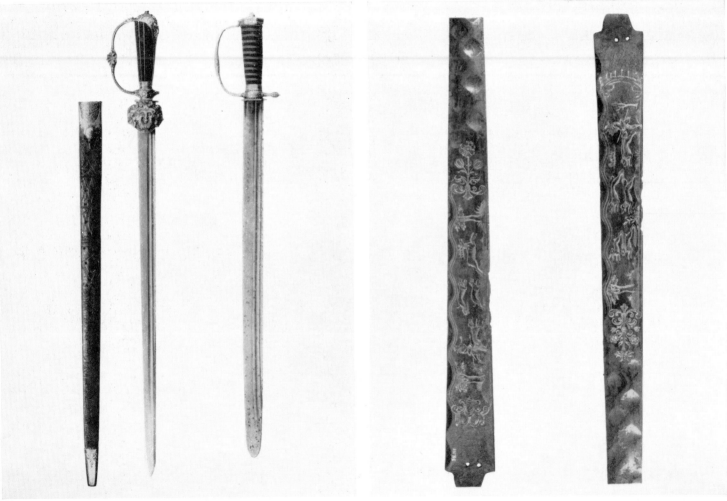

21

22

A   B

Plate 23 Four Hounslow sword-hilts, showing characteristic forms of the pommel and grip (pp 34–36)

Plate 24 London hanger-hilt with silver decoration (p 32)

Plate 25 Hounslow hanger-hilt with silver decoration (p 37)

Plate 26 Gilt bronze hilt, late 17th century (p 33)

C   D

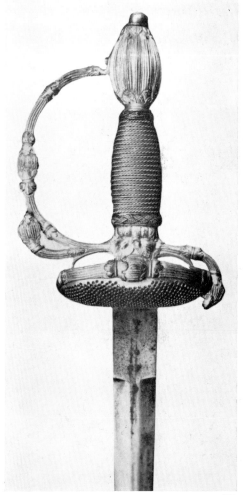

A   B   C   D

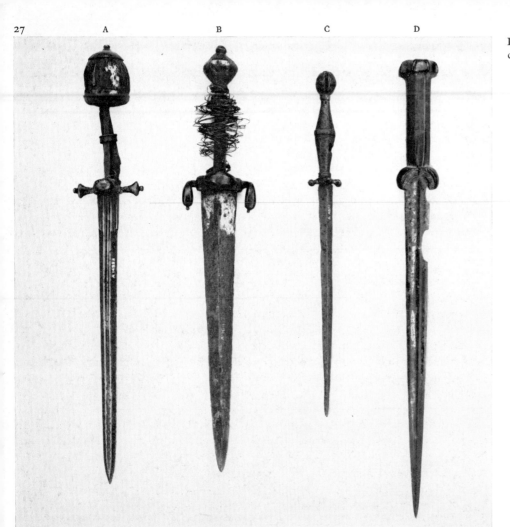

Plate 27 Daggers from London, 16th and 17th centuries (pp 37–39)

Fig. 3 Use of the two-handed sword in battle, from Holinshed's *Chronicles*

Rhine-province, and of Johann Conings or Coninck, possibly the 'John Counyne' of the Cutlers' Company records. Fleisch has turned his name into Latin, and signed his swords with the phrase 'Casper (*sic*) Carnis me fecit London', and the name of Peter Munsten, the maker of two of the other 'London' blades, is also associated with the sword given by Pope Clement VIII as a wedding-present to Henry IV of France.[1] A London-made blade bearing this name is in the Tøjhusmuseum at Copenhagen, and yet another is in the Livrustkammaren at Stockholm.

These four swords are of the familiar cup-hilted type worn in England in the first half of the seventeenth century. The cup is of saucer form, not the smooth hemisphere so popular in Italy and Spain and surviving in the modern *épée-de-combat*, and the two Munsten examples show an affinity with the later 'basket' hilt, as the cup or shell is prolonged at one side, dwindling finally about the middle of the knuckle-bow, and is pierced to allow the quillon to come right through it. The construction of such a hilt would seem, accordingly, to have been a matter of some ingenuity. The fifth sword shows a less well-known form of the cup-hilt. Here, the fingers and the *pas d'âne* are

[1] J.379, Musée de l'Armée, Paris. See Laking, *European Armour and Arms*, IV, 308, 310.

protected by a very slightly curved shell, of figure-of-eight shape and asymmetrical outline, chiselled on the outside with battle-scenes in high relief. Similar scenes, with masks and single equestrian figures, are to be observed on the pommel and the block that holds the quillons, the quillons themselves are formed like buxom young women bending provocatively sideways, and more cavalry engagements, in much lower relief, decorate the interior of the shell. The chiselling is bold to the point of crudity and suggests England or Holland in point of style, while the blade is signed JOHANNIS CONINGS (or CONINCK) LONDINI. This type is frequently known as a 'transition' rapier, and the uneven balance of the shell is a feature found in various other examples, notably the specimen illustrated on Plate CVIII of Meyrick and Skelton's *Engraved Illustrations of Antient Arms and Armour*, 1830. These swords would appear to have been worn about 1650-60, as successors to the cup-hilted type already described.

One other signed rapier, very similar in appearance to these Munsten swords, has a more definite local ascription, in that its place of origin is not called 'London' but 'Hounsloe'. It is dated 1635, and signed by Johan Kinndt, and is of particular interest as forming a link between the 'London'

walking-rapiers already mentioned and the 'service' swords made at Hounslow in the succeeding years.

A.1785
Large sword, with single-edged blade, straight quillons with mushroom ends, and one side-ring. Spherical pommel. Length over all, 28½ in. Late 15th century. From the Thames.
Given by Sir Guy Laking, Bart.

A.17462 (Plate 13)
Part of a sword. Single-edged blade, not set centrally in the hilt, but about half an inch towards the cutting edge. One quillon sharply curved, the other broken. Flat tang with four rivet-holes, one containing a double washer. Ends in a thistle-head, indicating the shape of the pommel. Probably a ceremonial weapon.
Late 15th or early 16th century. Found in London.
Given by W. J. Pavyer, Esq.

A.16991
Baselard, with single-edged blade, much corroded. Pommel, one quillon and part of tang missing. Short projection to guard the knuckles.
Early 16th century. From Hackney Brook.

A.20451 (Plate 17)
Sword of 'Landsknecht' type. Broad, double-edged blade 26½ in. long, with a triple groove running to the point, indicating that it has been cut down from a longer weapon. Characteristic fish-tail pommel with triple gilt rosette cap, and gilt escutcheon on collar, engraved with the Imperial eagle. Large figure-of-eight quillons with gilt knob terminals and pattern of raised gilt lozenges issuing from dragon or serpent heads. Short space for grip (missing) between pommel-

collar and quillon block. Traces of applied gilt cable ornament. See *Archaeological Journal*, XXXIII, 92. Laking, *European Armour and Arms*, II, 299. About 1520. Found on the site of New Scotland Yard, when digging the foundations for Mapleson's English Opera House (never completed), at a depth of 30 ft., in the silt and sand of the old foreshore.
Given by Edward Street, Esq.

39.50
Sword with broad double-edged blade much corroded, 27 in. long and 2¼ in. broad just before the root, where it is cut away and blunted to accommodate the forefinger. Double groove running nearly the whole length of the blade. Oblong quillon-block with single large side-ring and boldly curved quillons, one serving as knuckle-bow. Spheroidal pommel with short vaselike neck and terminal button.
Early 16th century. Found at Storey's Gate.

36.153 (Plate 15)
Two-handed sword. Broad, double-edged blade with armourer's mark on long ricasso, and small side-lugs to protect the forefinger. Straight quillons and heavy pommel. Length over all, 56 in. First half of 16th century. Found at Southall, when excavating for the Great Western Railway.

32.69
Rapier with long, rigid blade, double-edged, *pas d'âne* and side rings. Pommel detached. Traces of gilding on ricasso.
Third quarter of 16th century. Found when digging foundations in Great Peter Street, Westminster, at the corner of Strutton Ground. Possibly a relic of a duel in Tothill Fields.
Given by M. and R. Holmes.

A.10437 (Plate 16)
Sword with broad double-edged blade, broken at the point. Hilt with *pas d'âne*, quillons, knuckle-bow and large side rings. Pommel pierced for a sword-knot. Length over all, 40 in.
Late 16th century. Found in the making of the Thames Embankment. Illustrates the type of sword worn with armour in the reign of Elizabeth. The custom of piercing the pommel is rare before 1600.

A.7774
Rapier with blade 32½ in. long, inscribed OMAS YALA (for Tomas Ayala), long pommel, counter-curved quillons and open-work cup, much broken, with latticed lozenges and open panels. (It was not uncommon for blade-smiths to inscribe on their products the names of well-known makers, the most familiar example being the name 'ANDREA FERARA', found on Scottish broad-swords of the 18th century.)
Early 17th century. Found in Southampton Row.
Given by Felix Joubert, Esq.

A.2283
Rapier with plain blade 30½ in. long, fluted oval pommel, voluted quillons, scroll-ended knuckle-bow and open-work cup.
Early 17th century. Found in the roof of an old house in Westminster.
Given by Sir Guy Laking, Bart.

49.61/2
Rapier, much corroded, with flamboyant blade 30 in. long, deeply grooved in forte and bearing a crescent and a helmet-shaped mark on the ricasso. Fluted oval pommel, voluted quillons and open-work cup. Knuckle-bow riveted to pommel.

An excavated piece from an unrecorded site, but characteristically English and probably London-made.

35.150 (Plate 18A)
Rapier, with blade 35¼ in. long, inscribed CASPER CARNIS ME FECIT LONDON, fluted oval pommel, cylindrical wooden grip; counter-curved quillons and open-work cup with rosette-perforated centre and surrounding panels of strapwork. The maker, Caspar Fleisch, was a well-known blade-smith of Solingen.
Early 17th century. Formerly in the Seymour Lucas Collection.

52.59
Rapier, with blade 35¼ in. long, inscribed CASPER CARNIS FECIT LONDON. Twelve-sided oval pommel, grip formerly bound with copper wire, no knuckle-bow, voluted quillons in one piece with pierced steel cup with latticed pelta-like designs and scalloped border. The cup is shallower than those of the preceding examples, and approximates more nearly to those on the swords made by Peter Munsten.
About 1630.

36.119 (Plate 18B)
Rapier with blade 35¼ in. long, bearing orb-and-cross marks and inscribed PETER MVNSTEN ME FECIT LONDON. Vase-shaped pommel, grip covered with leather, voluted quillons and perforated cup with feathered border and extension over half the knuckle-bow.

Munsten was a well-known Solingen name. A Peter Munsten was Mayor of Solingen in 1597-98, and made the blade of the sword given as a wedding-present to Henry IV of France by Pope Clement VIII (J.379 Musée de l'Armée, Paris).

Other London-made blades bearing this name are at Copenhagen and Stockholm. See Laking, *European Armour and Arms*, IV, 308, 310.
Early 17th century.
Given in memory of the late Mrs. T. V. Wheeler, F.S.A.

36.154/1
Rapier (broken) with blade inscribed PETER MVNSTEN ME FECIT and PETER MVNSTEN LONDON, voluted quillons (one broken) and cup similar to the preceding, but nearly solid. Grip missing, and pommel not the original.
Early 17th century.
Given by the National Art-Collections Fund.

46.42 (Plate 24)
Hanger with curved single-edged blade 33¼ in. long, inscribed IOHANNIS BELL ME FECIT LONDON. Steel hilt with rear quillon, knuckle-bow (broken), flat pommel-cap with knob, and single trefoil shell turned over towards point and decorated with all-over fretted pattern of silver dots. Stag-horn grip. Black leather scabbard with lacquered brass locket-mount, stud and chape (probably later).

44.17 (Plate 19, left)
Cutlass or hanger, with serrated back, and straight single-edged blade 36¼ in. long set into silver hilt of about 1745. Rear quillon broken off, knuckle-bow notched into cap-and-spine pommel with small terminal knob, drop shell guard decorated with mask and scrolls. Similar mask on spine, scrolls on knuckle-bow and cap, and beaked mask on quillon-block. Dark leather scabbard with lozenge pattern of incised lines and perforations, and fitted with silver-plated brass mounts with grotesque tiger-like mask. Blade and scabbard

traditionally owned by Sir Thomas Player, City Chamberlain of London 1651-72.
Given by G. R. Brigstocke, Esq.

38.111 (Plate 20)
Blade of a hunting-sword, 25¼ in. long to shoulder, straight and single-edged, with undulating back, and design of hunting scenes inlaid in gold. Series of circular depressions running to the point, to continue the undulating effect.
Early 17th century. Found in Welbeck Street.

39.77
Blade of hanger, single-edged, 22¼ in. long. Broad tang, stamped with fleur-de-lys and the letters AM. Probably mid 17th century. Found on Hampstead Heath.
Given by F. J. Brown, Esq.

A.930
Hanger, with curved single-edged blade 18¼ in. long, marked with a crescent. Hilt with stag-horn grip, rear quillon and knuckle-bow fitted into cap-shaped pommel with pierced knob finial. 17th or 18th century. Found near Limehouse Church.

A.12992 (Plate 21)
Broadsword with straight single-edged blade 32¼ in. long, with running wolf mark and modern bluing and gilt inscription: '*This ancient sword, date of Charles I, was found by the Revd. J. Waldy in an old farm-house at Hungerford, and presented by the Baroness Burdett-Coutts to Mr. Henry Irving in 1878 in remembrance of his magnificent histrionic representation of that monarch.*'
  Silver-plated half-basket hilt with twin-shell guard; knuckle-bow set into large pommel, and two counter-guards. Grip bound with alternate thick and fine cabled silver wire. Shells and

pommel bear the device of a boar within the Garter, surmounted by an earl's coronet, the badge of Aubrey de Vere, 20th Earl of Oxford who in 1661 was Colonel of the Oxford Blues, subsequently the Royal Horse Guards (Blue). Probably an officer's sword of that regiment and date. The scabbard is modern.
Given by H. B. Irving, Esq.

A.5919
Cut-and-thrust sword with double-edged blade 31¾ in. long. Steel hilt with rear quillon, twin-shell guard, two scrolled counter-guards and knuckle-bow notched into domed pommel, the whole decorated with patterns of small silver rosettes. Shape of hilt closely resembles that of A.12992, the Horse Guards sword of 1661-62, and decoration recalls the earlier London-made hanger by John Bell, No. 46.42. Grip bound with thick and fine cabled copper wire.
Found in London.

A.13806 (Plate 22)
Transition rapier, with blade of lozenge section, 32 in. long, inscribed JOHANNIS CONINGS LONDINI in deep groove. Counter-curved quillons formed like young women, practicable *pas d'âne* and asymmetrical twin-shell guard. Guard chiselled with cavalry encounters on both sides, quillon-block with masks and mounted figures, and pommel with cavalry combats and female figures. Grip bound with copper wire. 1660-70.

A.1802
Transition rapier, with blade of lozenge section, 32 in. long. Short quillons, expanding at the ends into hollow latticed bulbs, broken on one side.

Lobated twin-shell guard, much bent, decorated with similar latticed panels. Grip spirally bound with copper wire in flat ribbon, fine and coarse cables. Round, hollow pommel with latticed panels (broken) and remains of similar panel on quillon-block.

1660-70. Found in London.

Given by Sir Guy Laking, Bart.

A.10793

Blade of a boy's sword, of diamond section.

Late 17th century. Found in the Kingsway.

A.11468

Sword-blade, straight and flat, with blunted edges and rounded point. Length only 19¾ in. over all. No appearance of ever having been sharp. Possibly a theatrical 'property'.

17th century. From the site of the Globe Theatre, Bankside.

R. E. Way Collection.

A.5918 (Plate 26)

Cut-and-thrust sword with double-edged blade 32½ in. long, engraved for practically all its length in the 18th or 19th century with leaf and flower patterns, trophies, a crown and apparently a G.R. monogram partly effaced. Gilt bronze hilt with sharply counter-curved quillons; knuckle-bow screwed into oval pommel, vertically ribbed and capped at each end by a small calyx of leaves. Pommel-design repeated in miniature on quillon-knobs and middle of knuckle-bow. Practicable *pas d'âne* and perforated twin-shell guard. Ricasso engraved with the word LONDON, normally hidden by the hilt. Grip re-wound in 1949 with silver wire from the original 'Turk's head' mounts. The scabbard is modern.

Late 17th century.

The Hounslow Sword Factory

In the year 1636 a certain Benjamin Stone advertised that he had perfected the art of blade-making, and that his factory at Hounslow produced blades 'as good cheap as any to be found in the Christian world'. He may have taken in hand the businesses previously run by Kinndt and Munsten, possibly changing their policy somewhat, as after this time the name of Kinndt is associated not with rapiers but with cavalry swords and naval cutlasses. Possibly the use of the name of Hounslow, in preference to the vaguer 'London', is also a mark of his re-organization.

A good many Hounslow blades bear no maker's name or date at all, but some show the 'running wolf' mark, with or without a date, and Kinndt's name appears on blades dated 1634 and 1635. Johannes Hoppie and Richard Hopkins also made swords with Kinndt, and in 1643 the factory had a strong enough reputation for an anonymous pamphleteer to allude to it as a suitable destination for the ironwork of Cheapside Cross,[1] and for General Waller to apply to Parliament for a purchase-grant for 'two hundred swords of Kennet's making of Hounslow'. The D of Kinndt's name is often so crudely inscribed that it could easily be misread as 'Kennet', and it would seem that Kinndt was the best known of the Hounslow workmen. It is, however, unlikely that the order was actually placed with him, as the Hounslow factory had Royalist sympathies and was accordingly suppressed, and the cutlers' contracts for Fairfax's New Model Army in 1645 specify the provision of *Dutch* blades at 4s. 6d. each.

As has been said, Hounslow swords are generally single-edged cavalry weapons for cut-and-thrust work, or curved cutlasses for use at sea. The backs of these latter are often serrated, like pioneers' swords and bayonets of a later day, to serve as saws amid dense undergrowth or jungle.[2] Hilts vary between the plain cross-hilt, with or without a shell to guard the knuckles, and the complete 'basket' type. Several examples show a lion-head pommel with a long collar extending well up the ribbed wooden grip. Hunting swords, or 'hangers', were also made at Hounslow. They resemble the cutlasses, but are more elaborately hilted. The shell, that in the cutlass spread out over the knuckles, is

reversed in the hanger and turned in the direction of the point, so as to hide the junction of hilt and blade, and to fulfil a decorative instead of a protective function.

One or two have been re-hilted in the eighteenth century. Notable examples are illustrated in Plate 19. One has a Hounslow blade made by Kinndt in 1634, in a silver hilt of at least a hundred years later, and the other is a very elaborate specimen which was supposed, by a tradition in the donor's family, to have belonged to Sir Thomas Player, City Chamberlain under Charles II. The blade and scabbard may well have been his. The sword has changed its character completely, however, by the substitution of an elaborate silver hilt that can be assigned, by the analogy of a dated example at the Tower, to 1745. The practice of wearing a hanger or hunting-sword instead of the more usual small-sword was followed by those who affected a quasi-military or naval style, like Roderick Random's pleasant but detrimental friend Beau Jackson, who had been a surgeon's second mate on board the *Elizabeth*, and whose silver-hilted hanger fetched two guineas at a pawnshop in 1739.[3]

[1] *The Downe-fall of Dagon* (anonymous tract), 1643.
[2] In the first scene of D'Urfey's *Commonwealth of Women* (1686), Boldsprite the shipmaster says, 'Captain, if you dare trust me in your Affair, they shall saw off my Beard with a Back-Sword, e're I leave you', which suggests that the serrated back was still in use.
[3] Smollett, *Roderick Random*, Chap. XVI.

It continued as part of the 'macaroni' fashions of the latter part of the century, and Shuter the comedian (1728-76) is cited by Planché as the last man to wear a hanger habitually in the London streets.

36.155/2 (Plate 23A)
Cutlass with serrated back, blade 25½ in. long, dated 1634 and marked with the running fox, a symbol occasionally found on Hounslow work. Hilt with open-work shell showing traces of silver plating and half-obliterated design of Neptune drawn by sea-horses; counter-curved quillons ending in small masks (the front one pierced through the jaws for a sword-knot), ribbed wooden grip and lion-head pommel as on many Hounslow examples.
Given by the National Art-Collections Fund.

36.154/4

Sword with straight single-edged blade 34 in. long, inscribed HOVN. ME FACIT. Lion-head pommel with deep coronet collar, ribbed wooden grip and broad shells coalescing with scrolled rear quillon and flat knuckle-bow screwed into pommel.

36.154/6 (Plate 23B)

Cutlass with blade 27¾ in. long, inscribed ME FECIT HOVNSLO, two-barred hilt decorated with masks and traces of silver plating, ribbed horn grip and brass pommel with grotesque human face adorned with fillets, ram's horns, shell pattern and deep collar encircled by a marquis's coronet.
Given by the National Art-Collections Fund.

47.36/1

Sword with straight single-e ged blade 33⅜ in. long, inscribed ME FECIT HOVNSLO between crosses. Steel basket hilt with two counter-guards, all screwed into nearly spherical pommel. Shell and pommel decorated with broad single-line pattern. Semi-circular languets and rudimentary interior quillons holding basket-hilt in place.

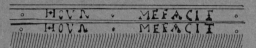

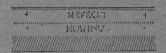

37.60 (Plate 19, right)

Cutlass with serrated back, blade 20¾ in. long, inscribed JOHAN KINNDT HOVNSLOE 1634. The blade has been much ground and re-set in a silver-plated 18th century hilt, with flat-capped pommel and grip of fish-skin bound with silver wire.

36.155/1

Cutlass with serrated back, blade 27¾ in. long, inscribed JOH(A)N KINNDT HOVNSLOE 1635. Large asymmetrical twin-shell guard, cylindrical grip bound with wire and plain knob pommel, with hole for end of knuckle-bow (broken).
Given by the National Art-Collections Fund.

37.74 (Plate 18C)

Rapier with blade 33¼ in. long, inscribed JOHAN KINNDT HOVNSLOE 1635. Hilt of the same pattern as 36.119, but no leather binding left on grip, and one quillon broken, perhaps by design, where it pierces the extension of the cup. Knuckle-bow screwed to pommel.

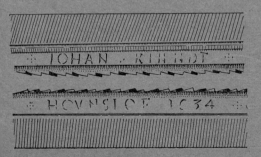

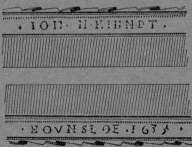

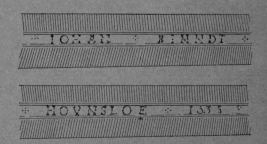

36.154/5 (Plate 23C)

Sword with straight single-edged blade 25¾ in. long, inscribed ME FECIT HOVNSLOE. Iron lion-head pommel with deep collar, ribbed wooden grip and broad shells chiselled with masks and joined to quillons by horizontal counter-guards. Knuckle-bow expanding into a shell and screwed to pommel. The grooving of the blade continues to the point, showing that it has been broken and reground.

36.154/2 (Plate 18D)

Sword of 'mortuary' type. Straight single-edged blade 35½ in. long, inscribed ME(FEC)IT HVNSLOE. Basket hilt with featherwork pattern, possibly derived from the type seen in 36.119 and 37.74, and lining of red cloth. Knuckle-bow and two counter-guards all screwed into mushroom pommel with feather-work decoration.

Given by the National Art-Collections Fund.

36.154/3

Sword with straight single-edged blade 32¼ in. long, inscribed ME FECIT HOUNSLOE. Fish-skin grip bound with wire, and basket hilt with external finger-guard and loop for picking up the bridle, though the former is rendered impracticable by the leather lining.

Given by the National Art-Collections Fund.

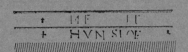

53.50 (Plate 23D)

Broadsword with straight double-edged blade 26¼ in. long, inscribed with orb and cross and MADE IN HOVNSLOE BY IOANNES HOPPIE FOR RICHARD BRIGINGSHAW 1636. Steel half-basket hilt with perforated shells and small languets, two scrolled counter-guards and knuckle-bow riveted into ribbed cylindrical pommel. Rear quillon ribbed to correspond. Fish-skin grip. Knuckle-bow broken just short of rivet.

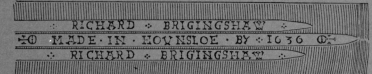

49.61/1

Sword with straight single-edged blade 33 in. long, inscribed ME FECIT HOVNSLO. Large iron hilt with volute-ended quillons, knuckle-bow formerly notched into pommel, and half-basket with asymmetrical shells, the smaller one broken away from its outer counter-guard. Grip bound with single and cabled copper wire alternately. Large egg-shaped pommel, outer side decorated with incised chevrons as on corresponding shell.

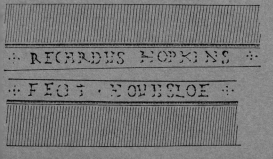

36.164/3 (Plate 25)

Hanger or hunting-sword, with curved single-edged blade 27¼ in. long, inscribed RECARDVS HOPKINS FECIT HOVNSLOE. Flat rear quillon, scrolled, and knuckle-bow screwed into scroll of flat pommel. Fish-skin grip bound with wire and silver-plated outer shell turned towards the point, forming a decoration rather than a practical covering for the hand. Inner shell probably broken, and finished off in a crude straight line.

Daggers

As with the sword, we find certain defensive features incorporated in the daggers of the sixteenth and seventeenth centuries. In addition to the quillons, an ungauntleted hand needed something at right angles to them, to protect the knuckles when the weapon was held point upwards, as it habitually was in fighting. Accordingly the hilt in the sixteenth century is equipped with an additional defence, sometimes a short projection like a vestigial quillon, but more ordinarily a stout, open ring, which would give the necessary amount of protection without unduly adding to the weight of the weapon.

An unusually early example of this is Plate 27A, a dagger found in the Thames at Westminster. The form of the blade, and the large wooden pommel inlaid with silver, suggest the 'Landsknecht' style of about 1520, but the hilt is equipped as well with a small side-ring which comes over the knuckle when the weapon is held in the hand, and provides the amount of projection necessary to protect the knuckle in the course of a parry. Sometimes the quillons themselves are given an additional function, as in Plate 27B, where they are given a double bend, first outwards from the blade and then sharply towards the point, as the illustration shows. An opponent's blade, on being parried, can be caught and held, for a moment at least, between the dagger-blade and the recurved quillons, giving greater facility for the riposte. The wood of the grip has rotted and fallen away, but the wire binding remains, and traces of gilding at the root of the blade show that the specimen must have been, in its day, a weapon of some pretensions. A blade of the same form, with similar gilding, was found in making the Thames Embankment, and is preserved in the Guildhall Museum, but the present example was recorded by the donor merely as having come from London.

In parrying with the left hand, a very small projection will suffice to make an angle that can catch and check a sliding blade, and Plate 27C, a dagger from Millbank, has no more than a short spur-like point over the knuckles. The general style of the excavated examples, however, indicates that the ordinary London dagger had a side-ring about an inch across.

Variations of these forms occur now and then. Sometimes we find a dagger with good blade and hilt but no side-defences at all. Sometimes, again, the hilt follows the orthodox lines, but the blade is so blunt, and the general workmanship so clumsy, that we may suspect we have to do with a toy or a theatrical 'property', as with various examples from London and Westminster. Occasionally, on the other hand, a specimen is found in which the craftsmanship of the sixteenth century has been applied to a form current in the Middle Ages. Such an example is Plate 27D, a dagger of the familiar 'kidney' type, so-called from the two lobes at the root of the blade. In its fifteenth-century form the grip is round, gradually swelling out to an almost flat pommel, but in later examples, of which this is one, the grip and pommel are in one piece, of polygonal section, and the pommel is mushroom-like, sometimes ending in a small metal setting for a jewel. Tradition says that this particular specimen had such a finial at the time of its discovery, but it had been detached and lost before the weapon came into the possession of the Museum. Recent investigation has revealed a quantity of floriated engraving at the root of the blade, and a maker's mark in the form of the letter M in copper. A dagger of the same type, with similar decoration

and apparently the same mark, was exhibited to the Society of Antiquaries in February 1888, and is illustrated in Laking's *Record of European Armour and Arms* (Vol. III, p 42) where its date is placed at approximately 1540. The decoration of the Museum dagger is badly affected at one point by corrosion, but the figures . . 56 appear to be traceable suggesting that this, like the weapon illustrated by Laking, may be reasonably assigned to the middle of the sixteenth century.

A.14993 (Plate 27A)
Dagger of 'Landsknecht' type, 14¾ in. long over all. Double-edged blade with armourer's mark M. Quillons and small side-ring set into an oblong block, with traces of gilding. Short grip with fragment of the original wood. Beehive pommel of wood with iron cap and traces of gold and silver decoration.
Early 16th century. From the Thames at Westminster.

48.9 (Plate 27D)
Dagger of 'kidney' type, 15½ in. long over all. Blade of lozenge section, much corroded but bearing traces of floriated engraving and a maker's mark M in copper. Traces of what may have been the date 15/56, half obliterated by corrosion. Ebony hilt in one piece, with kidney-like lobes on shoulders, octagonal grip and octagonally fluted mushroom pommel. Round mark on apex of pommel suggests the former presence of a finial, covering the end of the tang,

and tradition reports that the specimen, when excavated, had a small jewel in this position.
Mid 16th century. Found on the site of Salisbury House, London Wall.
Given by Gordon C. Reeves, Esq.

A.26276
Dagger, 17½ in. long over all, with single-edged blade of lozenge section, ribbon quillons and flat pommel, grooved at the sides. Maker's mark

is inlaid in copper on both sides of the blade, and a small rose is stamped on one quillon. Traces of engraving at root of blade on one side. Early 16th century. From the Thames at Temple Stairs.

A.26277
Dagger, 14½ in. long over all, with double-edged blade of lozenge section, heavy quillons curving sharply to point, boldly segmented and ending in 'wrythen knops' like those of contemporary spoons. A similar but larger knop forms the pommel. Grip missing.
Early 16th century. From the Thames at Temple Stairs.

A.16827 (Plate 27B)
Parrying-dagger, 14½ in. long over all. Double-edged blade ornamented with gilding. Side-ring and quillons set in oblong block; quillons bent sharply outward before turning toward the point. Grip missing, but binding of cabled copper wire still in position on tang. Hexagonal knob pommel.
16th century. Found in London.
Given by F. Ransom, Esq.

A.4951 (Plate 27C)
Parrying-dagger, 11¾ in. long over all. Double-edged blade of lozenge section. Diminutive knob quillons with sharp side-point. Hollow steel grip, swelling in the middle and encircled by three collars. Spherical pommel, with four deep vertical grooves, and decoration of rows of small crescents, facing alternate ways, as in the conventional representations of mail.
Late 16th century. From Millbank.

A.25639
Parrying-dagger, 11 in. long over all, with blade grooved on one side and ridged on the other.
Tang marked

Open-work ball pommel with figures of griffins.
Mid 16th century. Found in London.

A.6478
Parrying-dagger, 19½ in. long over all, with stout blade of lozenge section, with ricasso. Side-ring and quillons broken off. Ball pommel. Whole specimen very much corroded.
Late 16th century. Found on the site of Marylebone Station.
Given by Sir Harry Waechter, Bart.

A.7876
Dagger (much bent), 15¼ in. long over all. Double-edged blade, quillons and fragment of side-ring set in oblong block, crown-shaped iron collar round tang, to hold a grip. Pear-shaped pommel.
Late 16th century. Found in Hammersmith.
Given by Hugh Sadler, Esq.

A.1954
Dagger, 15¾ in. long, similar to preceding, but quillons and side-ring broken off and blade much corroded.
Late 16th century. From the Thames at Westminster.
Given by Felix Joubert, Esq.

A.17925
Dagger, 13¾ in. long over all. Double-edged blade of lozenge section with traces of gilding, side-ring concreted into a shell, one quillon missing.
Late 16th century. From the Thames.
Given by W. Sharpe Ogden, Esq., F.S.A.

A.15304
Dagger, 9 in. long over all, with flat, blunt blade and rounded point. Probably a toy or theatrical 'property'. Side-ring, curved quillons and wire binding on grip.
16th century. From Bloomfield Street.

A.17635
Dagger, 9⅛ in. long over all, with double-edged blade, and hilt of poor workmanship, with cherub-heads on pommel and quillons. Wire binding still on grip.
16th century. Found in London.

A.17593
Part of dagger. Double-edged blade with ricasso, brass hilt with open-work crown-shaped finials to pommel and quillons. Wire binding on grip.
16th century. Found in Dartmouth Street.

Published by

HER MAJESTY'S STATIONERY OFFICE
To be purchased from
49 High Holborn London WCI
13A Castle Street Edinburgh EH2 3AR
109 St Mary Street Cardiff CFI IJW
Brazennose Street Manchester M60 8AS
50 Fairfax Street Bristol BSI 3DE
258 Broad Street Birmingham I
7 Linenhall Street Belfast BT2 8AY
or through any bookseller

First published 1957
Second edition 1970

SBN II 290062 3

Printed for Her Majesty's Stationery Office by
Lonsdale & Bartholomew Printing Ltd, Leicester,
England   Dd. 153225   K48